RECORD BREAKERS
HOCKEY

Blaine Wiseman

MEDIA ENHANCED BOOKS
AV2 BY WEIGL
ADDED VALUE • AUDIO VISUAL

D0897530

www.av2books.com

AV² by Weigl brings you media enhanced books that support active learning.

AV² provides enriched content that supplements and complements this book. Weigl's AV² books strive to create inspired learning and engage young minds for a total learning experience.

Go to **www.av2books.com**, and enter this book's unique code. You will have access to video, audio, web links, quizzes, a slide show, and activities.

BOOK CODE

S708682

Audio
Listen to sections of the book read aloud.

Video
Watch informative video clips.

Web Link
Find research sites and play interactive games.

Try This!
Complete activities and hands-on experiments.

Due to the dynamic nature of the Internet, some of the URLs and activities provided as part of AV² by Weigl may have changed or ceased to exist. AV² by Weigl accepts no responsibility for any such changes. All media enhanced books are regularly monitored to update addresses and sites in a timely manner. Contact AV² by Weigl at 1-866-649-3445 or av2books@weigl.com with any questions, comments, or feedback.

Published by AV² by Weigl
350 5ᵗʰ Avenue, 59ᵗʰ Floor
New York, NY 10118
Website: www.av2books.com   www.weigl.com

Library of Congress Cataloging-in-Publication Data

Wiseman, Blaine.
 Hockey / Blaine Wiseman.
    p. cm. -- (Record breakers)
 Includes index.
 ISBN 978-1-61690-112-7 (hardcover : alk. paper) -- ISBN 978-1-61690-113-4 (softcover : alk. paper) -- ISBN 978-1-61690-114-1 (e-book : alk. paper)
 1. Hockey--Records--Juvenile literature. I. Tait, Leia. II. Title.
 GV847.5.W58 2011
 796.962--dc22
                                2010006155

Printed in the United States of America in North Mankato, Minnesota

062010
WEP264000

Project Coordinator Heather C. Hudak
Design Terry Paulhus

Photo Credits
Every reasonable effort has been made to trace ownership and to obtain permission to reprint copyright material. The publishers would be pleased to have any errors or omissions brought to their attention so that they may be corrected in subsequent printings.

Weigl acknowledges Getty Images as its primary image supplier for this title.

Contents

The Players

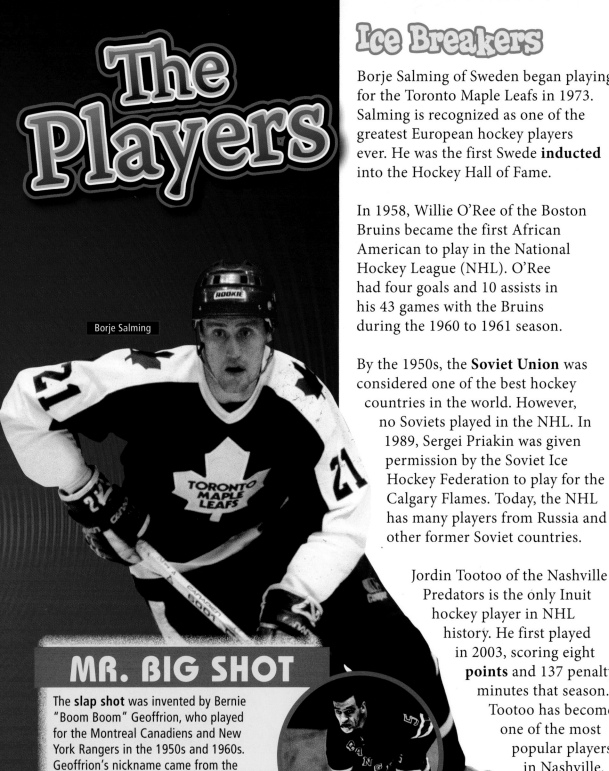

Borje Salming

Ice Breakers

Borje Salming of Sweden began playing for the Toronto Maple Leafs in 1973. Salming is recognized as one of the greatest European hockey players ever. He was the first Swede **inducted** into the Hockey Hall of Fame.

In 1958, Willie O'Ree of the Boston Bruins became the first African American to play in the National Hockey League (NHL). O'Ree had four goals and 10 assists in his 43 games with the Bruins during the 1960 to 1961 season.

By the 1950s, the **Soviet Union** was considered one of the best hockey countries in the world. However, no Soviets played in the NHL. In 1989, Sergei Priakin was given permission by the Soviet Ice Hockey Federation to play for the Calgary Flames. Today, the NHL has many players from Russia and other former Soviet countries.

Jordin Tootoo of the Nashville Predators is the only Inuit hockey player in NHL history. He first played in 2003, scoring eight **points** and 137 penalty minutes that season. Tootoo has become one of the most popular players in Nashville. He wears number 22, or two two.

MR. BIG SHOT

The **slap shot** was invented by Bernie "Boom Boom" Geoffrion, who played for the Montreal Canadiens and New York Rangers in the 1950s and 1960s. Geoffrion's nickname came from the sound made by his **slap shot**. The first "boom" was for the sound of his stick hitting the puck. The second "boom" stood for the sound of the puck flying into the boards.

Women on the Ice

In 1992, Manon Rheaume became the first woman to play professional hockey. She played goal in an exhibition game for the Tampa Bay Lightning. Rheaume earned her first professional win playing for the Knoxville Cherokees in the East Coast Hockey League (ECHL).

Manon Rheaume

Hayley Wickenheiser was invited to the Philadelphia Flyers' training camp in 1998 and 1999. Although she did not make the team, Wickenheiser became the first woman to score a goal for a men's professional hockey team when she joined the HC Salamat team of the Finnish Mestis Hockey League.

Hayley Wickenheiser

★ THE GREAT ONE ★

When Wayne Gretzky retired from the NHL in 1999, he held more than 60 records. In fact, he holds the record for breaking the most records. Here are some of Gretzky's record-breaking statistics.

Most career points – 2,857
Second place is held by Mark Messier, who has 970 fewer points than Gretzky.

Most career goals – 894
In 1994, Gretzky broke Gordie Howe's record of 801 career goals.

Most career assists – 1,963
Gretzky scored more assists in his career than any other player scored total points.

Most goals in one season – 92
Gretzky also holds the number two spot for most goals in one season, with 87. Brett Hull holds the number three spot, with 86.

Most points in one season – 215
Gretzky is the only player to score more than 200 points in one season, and he did it four times.

50 goals in 39 games – It was considered the greatest record in hockey when Maurice "The Rocket" Richard scored 50 goals in the first 50 games of the 1943 to 1944 season. In 1981, Gretzky broke the record by scoring 50 goals in only 39 games. Of all his records, Gretzky has said this one will be the hardest for another player to break.

Wayne Gretzky

5

The Goalies

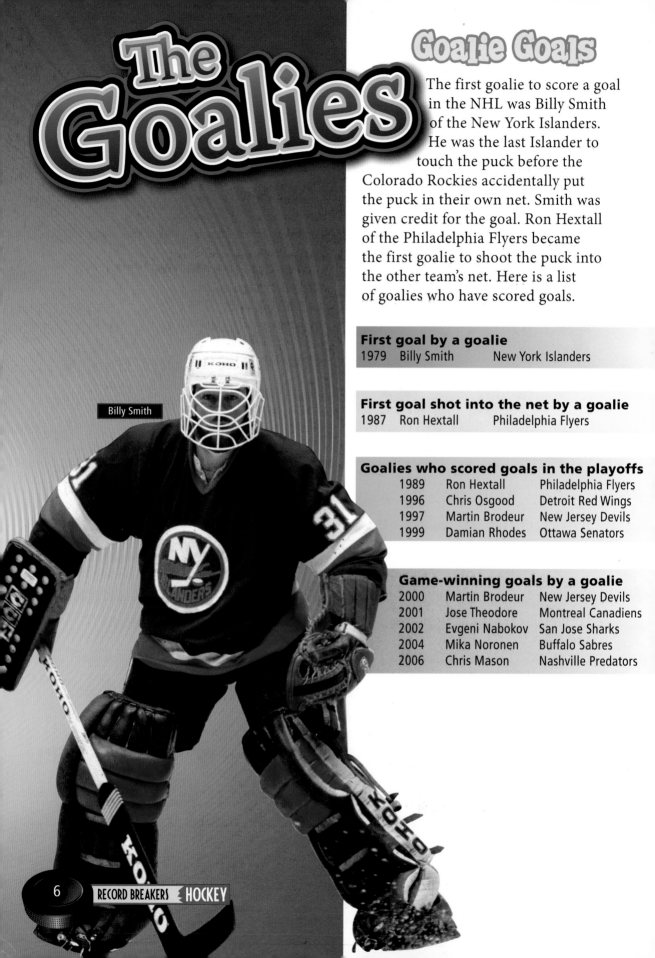

Billy Smith

Goalie Goals

The first goalie to score a goal in the NHL was Billy Smith of the New York Islanders. He was the last Islander to touch the puck before the Colorado Rockies accidentally put the puck in their own net. Smith was given credit for the goal. Ron Hextall of the Philadelphia Flyers became the first goalie to shoot the puck into the other team's net. Here is a list of goalies who have scored goals.

First goal by a goalie

1979	Billy Smith	New York Islanders

First goal shot into the net by a goalie

1987	Ron Hextall	Philadelphia Flyers

Goalies who scored goals in the playoffs

1989	Ron Hextall	Philadelphia Flyers
1996	Chris Osgood	Detroit Red Wings
1997	Martin Brodeur	New Jersey Devils
1999	Damian Rhodes	Ottawa Senators

Game-winning goals by a goalie

2000	Martin Brodeur	New Jersey Devils
2001	Jose Theodore	Montreal Canadiens
2002	Evgeni Nabokov	San Jose Sharks
2004	Mika Noronen	Buffalo Sabres
2006	Chris Mason	Nashville Predators

Mr. Goalie

Known as "Mr. Goalie," Glenn Hall played 18 seasons in the NHL between 1952 and 1971. He holds the record for most consecutive games played. Hall played in 502 straight games. This is equal to about eight straight seasons without missing any games. Hall's record is considered unbreakable. He was so nervous about playing that he would vomit before every game he ever played.

Glenn Hall

Shut the Door

A shutout is very important in hockey. It happens when the goalie stops every shot in a single game. During a game, if the opposing team has not scored, it is considered bad luck for a player to say the word "shutout." If a player says "shutout" and the other team scores, the player who said the word will be blamed for ruining the goalie's shutout.

These goalies have had the most NHL shutouts.

110 – **Martin Brodeur**, New Jersey Devils

103 – **Terry Sawchuk**, Detroit Red Wings, Boston Bruins, New York Rangers, Los Angeles Kings

94 – **George Hainsworth**, Montreal Canadiens, Toronto Maple Leafs

84 – **Glenn Hall**, Detroit Red Wings, Chicago Blackhawks, St. Louis Blues

82 – **Jacques Plante**, Montreal Canadiens, New York Rangers, St. Louis Blues, Toronto Maple Leafs, Boston Bruins

Marvelous Marty

Martin Brodeur holds several NHL records. He is considered among the greatest goalies of all time.

Most career wins – 602

Most wins in a season – 48

Most games played by a goalie – 1,076

Most shootout wins – 34

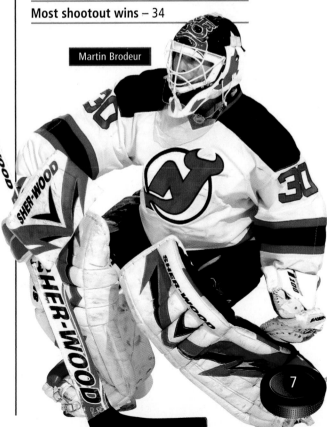

Martin Brodeur

Stripes and Strategies

Whistle Blowers

NHL officials have a difficult job. Referees and **linesmen** are booed by fans, hit by flying pucks, crunched between bodies, and required to break up fights. Here are some records held by NHL officials.

Kerry Fraser

Ray Scapinello

Most games refereed – 1,804
Kerry Fraser is known for his keen eye for penalties and his no-nonsense attitude. Fraser is also known for his slick hairdo, which never changed in more than 30 years.

Most consecutive games, linesman – 2,500 – Ray Scapinello is considered the Wayne Gretzky of linesmen. Nicknamed Scampy, he is the greatest linesman in NHL history. Scampy broke several records in his 33-year NHL career, including never missing a single game.

Leading the Charge

Scotty Bowman coached for 30 seasons in the NHL and is considered the greatest hockey coach of all-time. Bowman won more than 65 percent of his NHL games. This is more than any other coach in history. Bowman also holds the record for most losses in NHL history.

Known as a tough, serious coach, Bowman was respected, but not always liked, by his players. Steve Shutt once said, "You hated him 364 days a year, and on the 365th day, you got your Stanley Cup ring."

Bowman now works as an advisor to his son Stan Bowman, the general manager (GM) of the Chicago Blackhawks.

Scotty Bowman

Here are some of Bowman's records.

Most regular season games coached – 2,141

Most playoff games coached – 353

Most regular season wins – 1,244

Most playoff wins – 223

Most Stanley Cups won by a coach – 9

| 1973 | 1976 | 1977 | 1978 | 1979 | 1992 | 1997 | 1998 | 2002 |

Masterful Management

General managers have one of the most important jobs in hockey. They put the team together by making trades, signing **contracts**, and **drafting** young players.

The most successful GM in history is Sam Pollock. He won nine Stanley Cups with the Montreal Canadiens in the 1960s and 1970s. Pollock has also managed Team Canada and the Toronto Blue Jays baseball team.

Sam Pollock

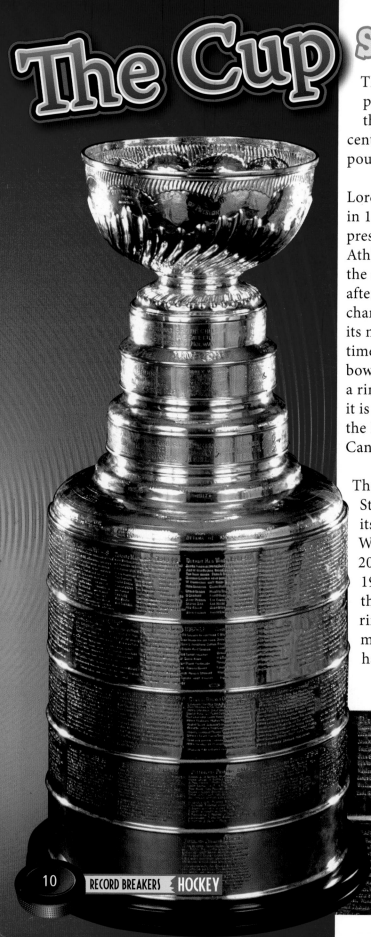

The Cup

Sizing It Up

The Stanley Cup is the largest professional sports trophy in the world. It stands 3 feet (91.4 centimeters) tall and weighs 34.5 pounds (15.6 kilograms).

Lord Stanley of Preston bought the cup in 1892 for about $50, and it was first presented to the Montreal Amateur Athletic Association in 1893. Originally, the cup was only a bowl. However, after winning the Stanley Cup, each championship team has the names of its members **engraved** on the cup. Over time, layers, or rings, were added to the bowl to make room for the names. When a ring of the cup is filled with names, it is removed and placed on the wall at the Hockey Hall of Fame in Toronto, Canada. A ring takes 13 years to be filled.

There are more than 2,000 names on the Stanley Cup. The first team to engrave its members' names was the Montreal Wanderers in 1907. The team added 20 names on the inside of the bowl. In 1925, the Victoria Cougars engraved the names of its members on the first ring on the outside of the cup. The members of each championship team have added their names ever since.

Name Game

Players, coaches, management, and staff can all have their names engraved on the Stanley Cup. However, there are rules about which teammates are included. To be listed on the cup, players must appear in at least 41 of the team's regular season games or in at least one game of the Stanley Cup finals. Teams can get special permission to add the names of players who were injured or sick and could not meet the requirements. Each team adds about 50 names to the cup when they win.

Travel Mug

The Stanley Cup is the only professional sports trophy that travels the world with the champions.

Each winning player gets to take the cup for one day during the offseason. It has been taken on trips to the White House and the Kremlin in Russia.

The cup has climbed a mountain in Canada and has been taken to show sick kids in hospitals around the world. Events showcasing the cup have raised millions of dollars for charities.

Oops!

There are several spelling mistakes on the Stanley Cup. Jacques Plante won the cup with the Montreal Canadiens five years in a row

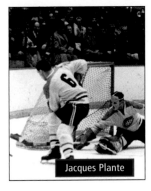
Jacques Plante

from 1956 to 1960. Each year, his name was spelled a different way. The misspellings include "Jock," "Jacque," "Plant," and "Plantes." In 1984, when the Edmonton Oilers won their first of five Stanley Cups, team owner Peter Pocklington had his father Bazil's name added to the cup. The name was later removed, and today, the letter "X" blocks out the name Bazil Pocklington.

★ CUP COLLECTORS ★

Henri Richard of the Montreal Canadiens holds the record for being the player with his name on the Stanley Cup the most times. Richard won 11 NHL championships in the 1950s, 1960s, and 1970s. Richard's teammates Jean Beliveau and Claude Provost are second, with

Henri Richard

10 cup wins each. However, Beliveau holds the record for most Stanley Cup championships overall. He won seven more Stanley Cups as a member of management.

The Gear

Craig MacTavish

Cricket and The Cat

At first, goalies did not wear special equipment. Over time, they began wearing padding to avoid injury. Goalies wore leg pads that were traditionally used by cricket players. These pads were much smaller than today's goalie pads. The first blocker and catcher were developed by Emile "The Cat" Francis of the New York Rangers in the 1943 to 1944 season. Francis used a baseball glove to catch the puck. He added a rubber sponge to another glove, which he used to block the puck.

Emile Francis

Watch Your Head

The first professional hockey player to wear a helmet was George Owen of the Boston Bruins in 1928. His helmet was made of leather. In 1968, Bill Masterton of the Minnesota North Stars died after he hit his head against the ice during a game. He was not wearing a helmet. In 1979, the NHL made a rule that all new players had to wear a helmet. The last person to play without a helmet was Craig MacTavish of the St. Louis Blues. MacTavish retired in 1996.

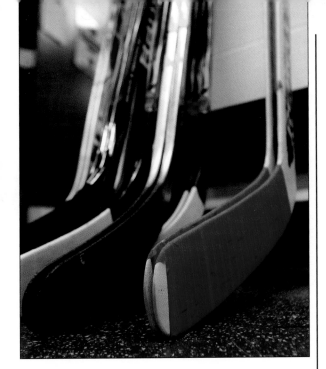

Stick it to 'Em

Today's hockey sticks are high-tech pieces of equipment made from lightweight, flexible, durable materials. When hockey was first played, sticks were heavy chunks of wood. They were carved from curved trees or branches. The oldest-known hockey stick in the world was carved in the 1830s from the roots of a maple tree.

Cold Potato

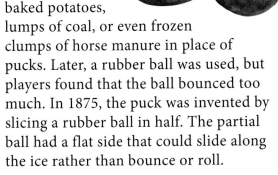

In the early years of hockey, players used frozen baked potatoes, lumps of coal, or even frozen clumps of horse manure in place of pucks. Later, a rubber ball was used, but players found that the ball bounced too much. In 1875, the puck was invented by slicing a rubber ball in half. The partial ball had a flat side that could slide along the ice rather than bounce or roll.

Masked Men

The first NHL goalie to wear a mask was Clint Benedict after he was knocked out by a slap shot to the head in 1929. Benedict only wore the bulky leather mask for a few weeks because he found it difficult to see the puck while wearing it. In 1959, Jacques Plante became the first goalie to wear a mask regularly. Before he wore a mask, Plante fractured his skull, broke his nose four times, broke both cheekbones, and broke his jaw.

Today's goalies are known for their painted masks. Painting masks became a tradition in the 1970s. Goalies choose their mask designs to represent their personality. Eddie "The Eagle" Belfour had a bald eagle on his mask for his entire career. Curtis "Cujo" Joseph's mask had a snarling dog that was inspired by the vicious dog in the Stephen King novel Cujo. The best-known goalie mask belonged to Gerry Cheevers of the Boston Bruins. In the 1970s, Cheevers wore a white mask, and each time a shot hit his face, he would draw stitch marks on the mask. By the end of his career, the mask was covered with thousands of stitch marks.

Gerry Cheevers

13

More Records

Before the Mask

Before they wore masks, goalies suffered terrible injuries. Lorne "Gump" Worsley once faced a slap shot from "The Golden Jet" Bobby Hull. The shot hit Worsley in the forehead, knocking him unconscious. Gump only wore a mask for the final six games of his career.

Terry Sawchuk was one of the greatest goalies of all time. Even before he played in the NHL, Sawchuk needed surgery to save his eye after being hit by a puck. During his NHL career, he received more than 600 stitches in his face.

Before he started wearing a mask, Don Simmonds had his eye knocked out of its socket. He also suffered 15 broken noses.

> " MY FACE IS MY MASK. "
>
> – Johnny Bower, goalie for the Toronto Maple Leafs from 1958 to 1969

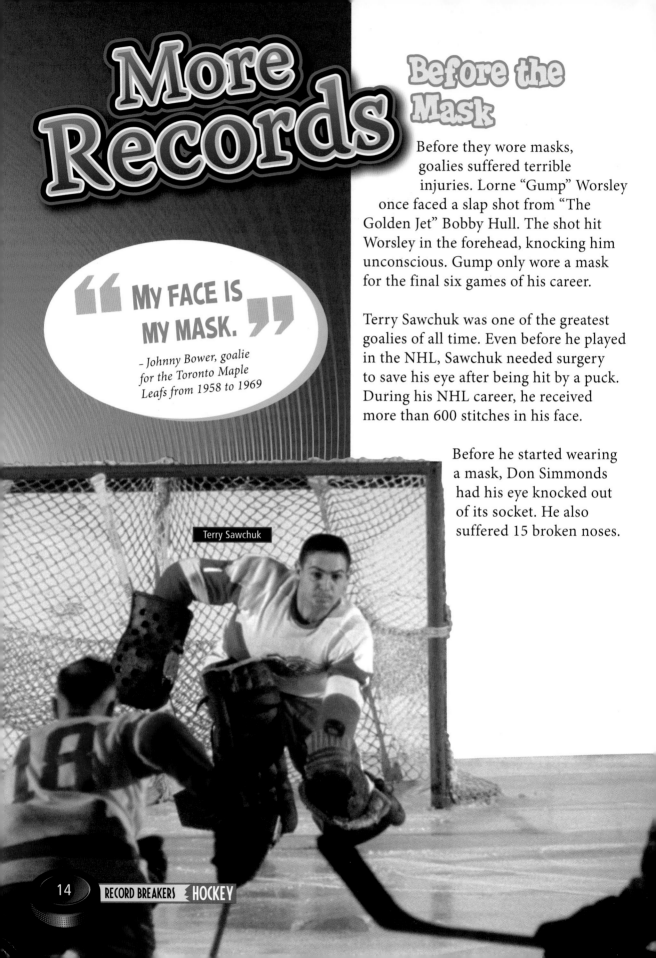

Terry Sawchuk

Long and Winding Road Trip

In 1904, the Dawson City Klondikers began the longest road trip in hockey history. They traveled by dogsled, bicycle, boat, and train across more than 4,000 miles (6,437 kilometers) from the Yukon to Ottawa. The team challenged the Ottawa Silver Seven, led by "One Eyed" Frank McGee, for the Stanley Cup. After the exhausting 25-day trip, the Klondikers lost the two games 9 to 2 and 23 to 2.

Ottawa Silver Seven

King of the Sin Bin

Hockey players must be in good physical shape. They play the fastest team sport in the world, and use their bodies to knock each other away from the puck. Sometimes, tempers flare and two players will fight. Players are put in the penalty box for fighting. Dave "Tiger" Williams holds the record for most penalty minutes. Williams was considered his team's "policeman," protecting the more skilled players. During his career, Williams spent 3,966 minutes in the penalty box. His NHL career featured more than 200 fights. He also scored 241 goals and 513 points in the NHL.

SCARS ON ICE

Clint Malarchuk

One of the most horrific injuries ever seen in the NHL happened to Clint Malarchuk of the Buffalo Sabres in 1989. While playing in goal, Malarchuk made an easy save as players rushed to the net. Steve Tuttle of the St. Louis Blues lost his balance. His skate left the ice and sliced Malarchuk's throat. The cut nearly killed Malarchuk, and it took more than 300 stitches to close the wound. After the incident, many goalies began wearing throat protection.

In 1986, Borje Salming was knocked down in a scramble for the puck. Gerrard Gallant of the Detroit Red Wings lost his balance and stepped on Salming's face with his skate blade. The blade sliced Salming from his forehead to his chin. He needed more than 250 stitches. Salming's teammate, Steve "Stumpy" Thomas, said Salming "looked like a softball after the game."

Borje Salming

15

All-time NHL Attendance Records

Average attendance at NHL games is usually between 18,000 and 20,000 people, but a few events have drawn larger crowds. Here are the NHL games with the highest all-time attendance.

Edmonton, Alberta

57,167

Commonwealth Stadium
November 22, 2003
Edmonton Oilers and
Montreal Canadiens

Chicago, Illinois

40,818

Wrigley Field
January 1, 2009
Chicago Blackhawks
and Detroit Red Wings

Pacific Ocean

Tampa, Florida

28,183

Thunderdome
April 23, 1996
Tampa Bay Lightning
and Philadelphia Flyers

N
W E
S

140 Miles
0   225 Kilometers

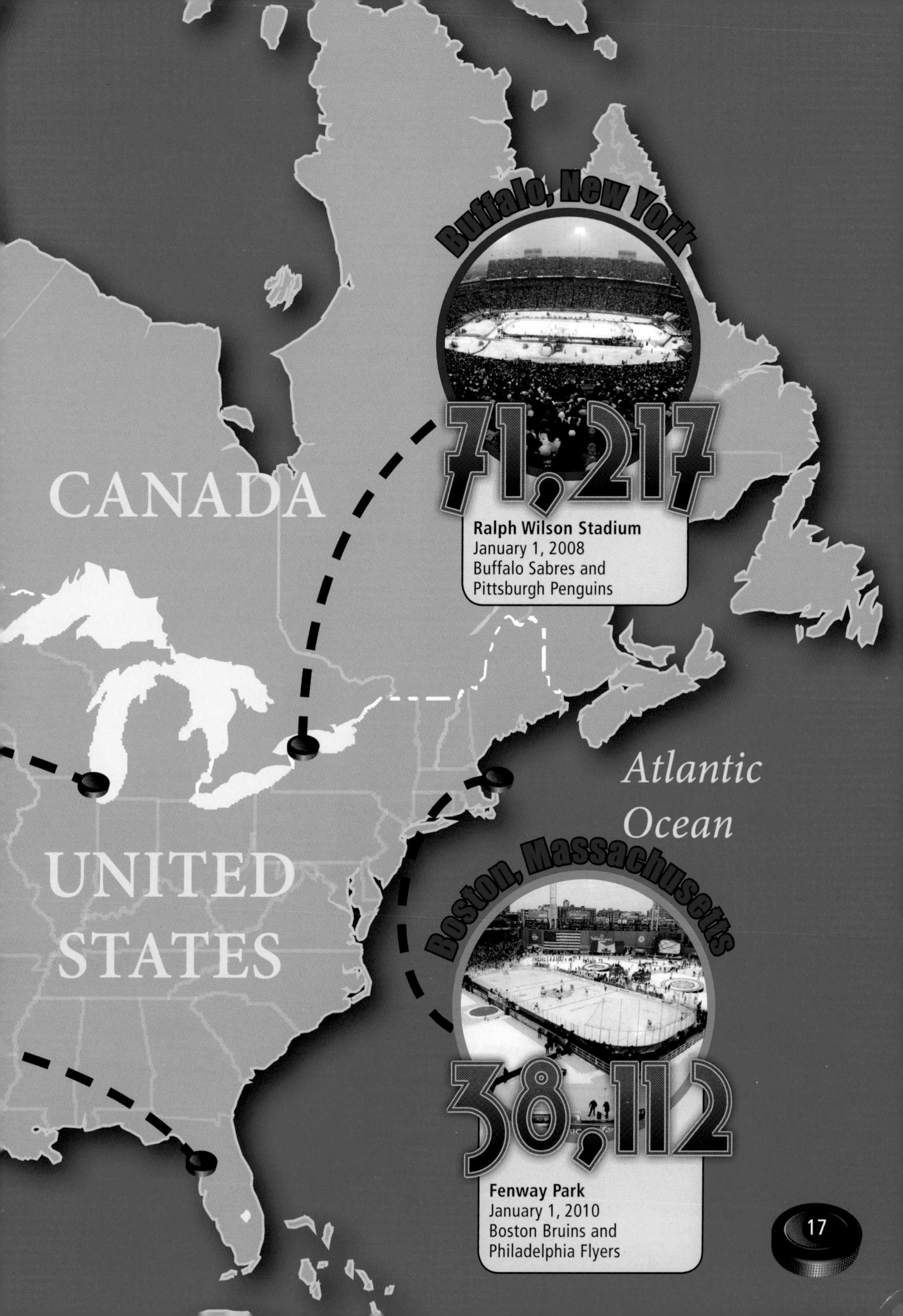

CANADA

Buffalo, New York

71,217

Ralph Wilson Stadium
January 1, 2008
Buffalo Sabres and
Pittsburgh Penguins

UNITED
STATES

Atlantic
Ocean

Boston, Massachusetts

38,112

Fenway Park
January 1, 2010
Boston Bruins and
Philadelphia Flyers

The Arenas

Pond Hockey

In 2003, the NHL went back to its roots. The Edmonton Oilers and Montreal Canadiens played an outdoor game at Commonwealth Stadium in Edmonton. It was the first time an NHL game had been played outdoors. A crowd of 57,167 people sat through a windchill of 5 degrees Fahrenheit to watch hockey legends, such as Wayne Gretzky, Guy Lafleur, and Mark Messier, play in a Legend's Game before the main event, The Heritage Classic. The Canadiens won the game 4 to 3.

In 2008, the NHL began a New Year's tradition, The Winter Classic. This is an annual outdoor game. The Buffalo Sabres played the Pittsburgh Penguins at Buffalo's Ralph Wilson Stadium, home to the Buffalo Bills football team. Sidney Crosby scored the winning goal in a shootout to beat the Sabres. The 2009 Winter Classic featured the Chicago Blackhawks hosting the Detroit Red Wings at the Chicago Cubs' baseball stadium, Wrigley Field. The Wings beat the Hawks 6 to 4. In 2010, the Boston Bruins beat the Philadelphia Flyers 2 to 1 at the legendary Fenway Park.

Wayne Gretzky

Guy Lafleur

Mark Messier

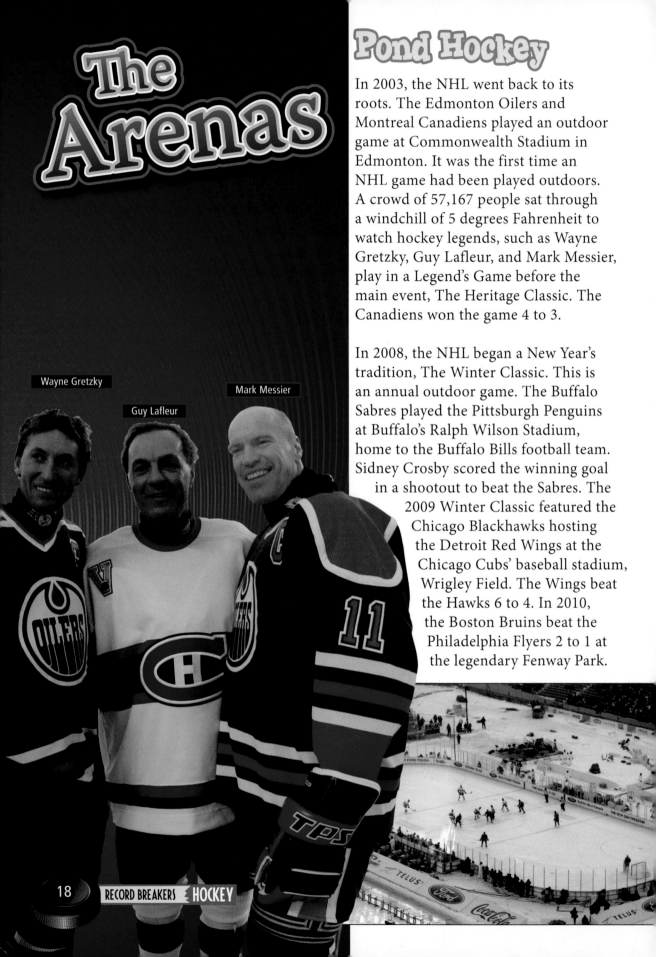

The Biggest Barns

Bell Centre – 21,273 seats
Home of the Montreal Canadiens
United Center – 20,500 seats
Home of the Chicago Blackhawks
Joe Louis Arena – 20,066 seats
Home of the Detroit Red Wings

Wachovia Center – 19,519 seats
Home of the Philadelphia Flyers
St. Pete Times Forum – 19,500 seats
Home of the Tampa Bay Lightning

The Original

Hockey began as an outdoor game. It was played on frozen rivers and lakes. Today, hockey is still widely played outside, but professional hockey is played in large, indoor stadiums. The first stadium built for hockey was the Montreal Forum in 1924. It was home to two NHL teams, the Canadiens and the Maroons. It cost $1.5 million to build and had 9,300 seats. The Canadiens became the greatest franchise in hockey while playing in the Forum. They played there until 1996.

THE GHOST OF THE FORUM

Howie Morenz was the first NHL superstar. Morenz was considered the greatest hockey player in the world when he played for the Montreal Canadiens in the 1920s and 1930s. He scored 270 goals and 467 points in the NHL, including playoffs. His career ended after he broke his leg during a game in 1937. The injury was so bad that Morenz said to his teammates, "I'm all through. This is the finish." Six weeks later, Morenz died from a blood clot caused by the broken leg. His funeral was held at the Montreal Forum, where 50,000 fans lined up to see his casket and more than 200,000 others lined the streets to pay their respects. Later, some people believed Morenz's ghost haunted the Forum. No other team seemed able to win the Stanley Cup playing at the Forum. Only one team defeated the curse. The Calgary Flames won the cup on Forum ice in 1989.

Howie Morenz

In The Money

BIG BUSINESS

NHL teams are businesses. People pay huge amounts of money to own NHL teams. These are the most valuable NHL teams.

Toronto Maple Leafs – $470 million

New York Rangers – $416 million

Montreal Canadiens – $339 million

Detroit Red Wings – $337 million

Philadelphia Flyers – $273 million

Rich Boys

NHL players are paid to play. The lowest paid NHL player earns $500,000 per year. However, the average salary is $2 million per year. Top players can be paid much more. These are the highest paid players in the NHL.

Vincent Lecavalier – $10 million per year
Tampa Bay Lightning

Sidney Crosby – $9 million per year
Pittsburgh Penguins

Evgeni Malkin – $9 million per year
Pittsburgh Penguins

Alexander Ovechkin – $9 million per year
Washington Capitals

Chris Drury – $8 million per year
New York Rangers

Spending at the Game

On average, how much do people spend at an NHL game?
Ticket: $50,
Hot dog: $4,
Soft drink: $4,
Program: $2.50,
Hat: $16

Vincent Lecavalier

NHL.COM

Culture

Harvey the Hound

Roast Duck

The Anaheim Ducks' mascot, Wild Wing, took part in the best-known NHL mascot moment. For his first stunt of the 1995 to 1996 season, Wild Wing tried to jump over a wall of fire by bouncing off a trampoline. His skate became stuck in the trampoline, and he fell into the fire. The mascot survived to continue entertaining hockey fans.

Coach Got Your Tongue?

Harvey the Hound was the first NHL mascot. Known for his red Calgary Flames hat and long tongue, Harvey leads loud cheers by banging a dog bone on a drum. Harvey's shining moment was in 2002, when the Flames were beating their **rivals**, the Edmonton Oilers, 4 to 0. Harvey was teasing the Oilers' players when coach Craig MacTavish turned and ripped Harvey's dangling tongue out of his mouth. MacTavish then threw the tongue into the crowd.

Eight Arms Lift the Cup

Detroit Red Wings fans take part in one of the most unusual traditions in all of sports. In 1952, the Wings needed to win eight games to win the Stanley Cup. A fan who owned a seafood shop threw an octopus onto the ice. The eight legs of the octopus represented the eight wins needed to claim the cup. The Red Wings won eight games in a row. The tradition continues today, with fans throwing octopuses that weigh as much as 50 pounds (23 kg) onto the ice.

QUIZ

1 Who was the first African American to play in the NHL?

2 Which goalie was the first to shoot the puck into the other team's net?

3 Which player's name appears on the Stanley Cup with five different spellings, five years in a row?

4 Which player holds the record for setting the most NHL records?

5 The ghost of which player is thought to have haunted the Montreal Forum?

ANSWERS: 1. Willie O'Ree 2. Ron Hextall 3. Jacques Plante 4. Wayne Gretzky 5. Howie Morenz

GLOSSARY

contracts: agreements between a player and a team regarding money

drafting: choosing young players to play for a team

engraved: carved words and numbers into an object

inducted: chosen to be a member

linesmen: hockey officials who work with referees

points: the sum of the number of goals and assists a player scores

rivals: two teams that dislike each other

slap shot: a powerful shot in which a player uses a hockey stick to slap the puck extremely hard

Soviet Union: a group of eastern European nations that were joined together in a union

INDEX

Log on to www.av2books.com

AV² by Weigl brings you media enhanced books that support active learning. Go to **www.av2books.com**, and enter the special code inside the front cover of this book. You will gain access to enriched and enhanced content that supplements and complements this book. Content includes video, audio, web links, quizzes, a slide show, and activities.

Audio
Listen to sections of the book read aloud.

Video
Watch informative video clips.

Web Link
Find research sites and play interactive games.

Try This!
Complete activities and hands-on experiments.

WHAT'S ONLINE?

Try This! Complete activities and hands-on experiments.	**Web Link** Find research sites and play interactive games.	**Video** Watch informative video clips.	**EXTRA FEATURES**
Pages 10-11 Try this hockey activity.	**Pages 6-7** Learn more about goalies.	**Pages 4-5** Watch a video about hockey.	**Audio** Hear introductory aud[...] at the top of every pag[...]
Pages 12-13 Test your knowledge of hockey gear.	**Pages 8-9** Read about coaches, managers, and referees.	**Pages 14-15** View stars of the sport in action.	**Key Words** Study vocabulary, and play a matching word game.
Pages 16-17 Complete this mapping activity.	**Pages 18-19** Find out more about where hockey games take place.	**Pages 20-21** watch a video about hockey players.	**Slide Show** View images and captions, and try a writing activity.
			AV² Quiz Take this quiz to test your knowledge